# Celebrations of
# A Mother's
# Love

## Real Stories from
## **Guideposts**® about Mothers
## and Their Children

Happy
Birthday!
We hope you
will enjoy this!
All our
love, Kevan
Roxann
Grant
& Rochelle
6-8-94

CRESCENT BOOKS
New York • Avenel, New Jersey

*Her children arise up, and call her blessed...*
—P<small>ROVERBS</small> 31:28

D id you know you owe your life to a real live heroine? Someone who put your needs before her own, even before you were born? In his book *The Power of Myth,* mythology expert Joseph Campbell discusses the heroism of motherhood, defined by its "giving over of oneself to the life of another." What a perfect description of what it means to be a mother!

My heroine ran along beside me on my first two-wheel bicycle ride, and together we tumbled into our neighbor's front yard. Later, she gave up a whole summer day and earned a body full of sore muscles putting together my first swing set. She never missed a school play or concert. When I was a teenager, she spent hours showing me how to curl my hair, then hours more doing it for me when I couldn't get it right. Now that I'm a mother, I know there were probably a dozen other things she would rather have been doing.

God asks us mothers what He asks of only His greatest heroes and heroines: to take complete responsibility for another's life. If it's true that a baby is God's way of saying the world should continue, to whom has He entrusted the care of that all-important link to the future? To mothers, of course.

So let's honor the heroines in our lives, the women who shape our world by molding its daughters and sons. Mothers deserve to be told that we know we'd be nothing without them.

—G<small>INA</small> B<small>RIDGEMAN</small>

*Heavenly Father, bless all mothers with the strength and wisdom to continue in the tough but most important job You've given them.*

*But Mary kept all these things, and pondered them in her heart.*
—LUKE 2:19

Of all the gifts God gave mothers, I'm most thankful that He created us with hearts made for *pondering*, just like Mary's. Shortly after the birth of Jesus, she must have felt exhausted with the accumulation of experiences . . . His dramatic delivery in that Bethlehem stable, and then all those shepherds arriving to tell her what the angels said about her Child. She couldn't possibly appreciate the meaning of each event, so she simply stored them away like treasures and *"pondered* them in her heart." Later, in Jesus' absence, this process of *pondering* must have become a source of comfort for her.

With two of our children in college and our youngest ready to reach for the car keys, I'm beginning to understand the comfort of *pondering* in their absence. When they were young, I often felt exhausted by their demands. I remember one day standing in the narrow checkout lane in the supermarket while all three made a final assault on the nearby candy rack. Surely, I looked like a frustrated octopus as I tried to catch hold of six hands at once. An older woman behind me smiled wistfully. "Enjoy these years," she said. "They pass *so* quickly." I thought she was loony.

But now that they're going their own ways, I understand better. She meant, "Store up all these experiences in your heart because some day in their absence, you'll *enjoy* all those treasures, without *any* of the fatigue and frustration."

So as I face these quieter times, I'm going to take time for *pondering*, appreciating the memory of all those great surprise breakfasts in bed (without enduring *any* burned toast crumbs under my pillow). What a gift!

—CAROL KUYKENDALL

*Lord, thank You for the gift of a heart made for pondering. And bless mothers everywhere for all that they give, all that they are.*

*Be still before the Lord . . . fret not yourself. . .*
—Psalm 37:7–8 (RSV)

When my daughter Ann was three, she found a picture of a troll in her storybook, and decided that he was living under her bed. She was so convinced of it, that night she refused to sleep in her room. "There's no reason to be afraid," I assured her. "There's no troll!" Nothing, however, could persuade her to get in her bed.

The hour grew late. I grew exasperated. The more I tried, the more insoluble the ridiculous problem seemed to get. So I threw up the parent's universal prayer: *"Help!"* Then I went to the kitchen to make cocoa, putting the whole thing out of my mind.

Ann and I were dropping marshmallows into our cups, when suddenly an idea popped into my head from out of the clear blue. While the troll wasn't real to me, it was very real to Ann, and I needed to acknowledge both her fear and the imaginary way she was projecting it. So as she watched, I reached under her bed, pulled out the invisible troll and tossed him out the window. "Thanks, Mama," she cried. Then she climbed in her bed and went to sleep. The troll never reappeared.

A small event, perhaps. But to this day, whenever I'm stymied by a problem, I remember what I learned that night: Very often God sends insights and solutions only when we stop fretting and become relaxed and still enough to receive Divine input.

—Sue Monk Kidd

*Dear God, when I've got a "troll" under my bed, teach me to turn aside for a while and listen.*

*I, Paul, write this greeting with my own hand.*
—I Corinthians 16:21 (rsv)

I keep this silly picture of my daughter Lindsay on my desk—her hair covered with confetti—to remind me to cover her with *long-distance love* this year while she's away at college. I snapped the picture just before hugging her good-bye at the end of a welcoming ceremony when clouds of confetti rained down on a roomful of jittery freshmen, a symbolic gesture of "covering them with love."

When I got home and looked at this picture, I began to think of the ways I could cover her with love . . . in spite of our physical separation. For ideas, I turned to the Apostle Paul, the "Master of Long-Distance Loving," who continually communicated comfort, encouragement and guidance to beloved new believers far away. According to Scripture, Paul used two main methods: He prayed for them regularly (and told them so); and he wrote letters. (Even today, I'll bet he'd choose writing over phoning because letters last longer.)

So I joined a Mothers' Prayer Group, which meets regularly to share requests and pray for our kids far away from home. And I purchased a supply of pre-stamped postcards and stationery for quick, regular notes, knowing that something—*anything*—fills an empty mailbox with a tangible message of love. Sometimes I tape a stick of gum to an index card ("I'm sticking with you!"), or send a picture postcard from Boulder (a "shot" of home), or tuck a local newspaper article in an envelope, or jot down a few "Proverbs from Mom" (starting with "Proverbs 32" since the Bible has 31). Obviously, my messages are not as deep as Paul's, but I hope my gestures of long-distance love are just as real.

—Carol Kuykendall

*Father, keep me faithful to "long-distance loving" as I enter this new phase of parenting.*

*Love goes on forever. . .*
—I CORINTHIANS 13:8 (TLB)

**M**y grandmother's pin is pale gold, embedded with twelve opalescent seed pearls. These glow from a crescent moon that tips upward to a shining star, with a little diamond that flickers light as from a secret hiding place, like whispered promises of dreams come true.

She wore it nearly always, on the small neat collar of a simple blouse or pinned askew on a sweater. She touched it sometimes, as though to pull from it faith and courage . . . to keep on dreaming.

Her wedding ring and the pin—that was all she had left in tangible remembrance of him. "He was my first and only love," she'd say about the grandfather I never knew.

Now the pin was mine. She gave it to me years ago folded in plain white tissue on which she had written in a shaky hand: "You are sweet sixteen—it's time for moonglow, dancing stars and promises of dreams come true!"

I have treasured it and worn it through the years, nearly always. Sometimes just tucking it into the dark recesses of a pocket, easy to the touch of my tired hands and tired heart, so much in need of promises.

A few years back, I wrapped the pin in plain white tissue on which I wrote to my daughter Katrelya:

> This Valentine's Day, my darling daughter, you are sweet sixteen—
> time for moonglow, dancing stars and the promises of dreams come
> true! Your great-grandmother's pin . . . wrapped in tissue . . .
> once given to me, now a token of remembrance and love passed
> along to you!

—FAY ANGUS

*Lord Jesus, as we share tokens of affection from our hearts with those we love, we remember that You are the Lover of our soul. Draw us close to Your heart.*

*The foolish ones said to the wise . . ."Our lamps are going out."*
—MATTHEW 25:8 (NIV)

"Hand me the lamp, young'un," Grandma said, reaching for the kerosene jug on the floor of the pantry.

I lifted the old lamp from its place on the shelf. Carefully Grandma removed the glass globe, trimmed the wick and began pouring kerosene into the base. "Got to keep her filled—just in case this newfangled stuff gives out," she'd say, waving at the light bulb overhead.

Often that "new stuff" did give out—when autumn storms shook the trees, when spring winds swept over our farm in wild fury. That's when Grandma would set that kerosene lamp in the center of the kitchen table, where its rays helped push back the darkness. And her satisfied smile was visible even in the dim light.

Sometimes I feel like I'm running out of "oil": I volunteer for one too many committees; I try to get by on a few hours of sleep; I forget to take my vitamins; I neglect reading my Bible; I convince myself that hot dogs really are nutritious. But soon I find I'm irritable and tired and discouraged. I snap at the kids, grumble when my husband Gary's late for dinner. I am less creative and more sarcastic. That's when I seem to hear Grandma saying, "Got to keep her filled." So I take time for a long walk in the woods or a leisurely bubble bath. I thumb through a magazine, treat myself to Mexican food, play checkers with my son Brett. I read the Gospels, pausing to hear the roar of the Sea of Galilee and the murmurs of surprise when Jesus heals the blind man. I turn my prayers into praises. And, like Grandma's kerosene lamp, I soon find I'm "filled up" and ready to shine!

—MARY LOU CARNEY

*Cure me, Father, of the emptiness caused by hurry and stress. Today I will stand still—and be filled.*

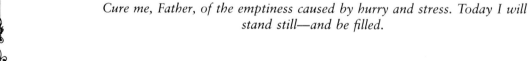

*Nevertheless I am continually with thee: thou hast holden me by my right hand.*
—Psalm 73:23

I missed my family when I remarried and moved to Oklahoma. It was always a joy to return to Georgia, which my husband and I did often. One day, while back in Georgia, my daughter Julie asked me to pick up four-year-old Katie at kindergarten. Sitting in the long line of cars waiting for my turn to drive by the school door, I recalled the countless times I had done the same thing for my four children.

Katie bounded out to the car, delighted to see me, and we drove off. I had to stop by the drugstore, and as Katie and I got out of the car, she immediately put her hand into mine. She seemed to do it without thinking or making a big deal of it. I'd forgotten what a wondrous thing it is to have a small, trusting hand thrust into your own. As we left the drugstore, once again her hand found mine. No words. Not even a glance. Just her hand securely nestled in mine.

Driving home I thought about the incident. *Why, God must feel exactly as I had!* What joy He must experience when with complete trust and without fanfare we simply slip our hand into His and walk alongside Him quietly and with absolute faith. It's a joy I want to extend this very day.

—Marion Bond West

*Right now, Father, I'll slip my hand into Yours as I go about my day.*

*. . . If a man is overtaken in any trespass, you who are spiritual*
*should restore him in a spirit of gentleness.*
—GALATIANS 6:1 (RSV)

It was past her bedtime. I'd told her not once, but three times to get into bed. But there she was, still sitting on the floor of her room, blowing up balloons and twisting them into assorted shapes. Earlier I'd bought my eleven-year-old daughter a "Balloon Craft" kit with a step-by-step instruction book on creating everything from a giraffe to a dachshund. She'd been captivated by it for hours to the point of ignoring me. Aggravated, I planted my fists on my hips. "Ann, get in bed and do it now!" I shouted.

She jumped. *Bam!* the blue balloon exploded in her hands. She stared at me as if her face, too, were about to shatter.

As she climbed into bed, I picked up the menagerie of balloons from the floor, then bent down to retrieve the book of instructions. That's when my eyes fell upon the bold print at the top of the page: "Twist and shape the figures *gently* to avoid popping."

I paused and looked at the little "figure" curled beneath the sheets. "I'm sorry I shouted at you," I whispered. Then I brushed back the brown bangs on her forehead ever so gently.

—SUE MONK KIDD

*Help me always to handle the lives around me with gentle, loving hands.*

ANTHONY DASILVA

*My children, our love is not to be just words or mere talk,*
*but something real and active.*
—I JOHN 3:18 (JB)

One Valentine's Day my daughter Rebecca handed me a slip of paper. "Look in the blue vase on your dresser," it instructed. I looked, and found another note: "See what's hidden in your jewelry box." A third note was wrapped around a necklace, this one directing me to reach under my pillow. I did, and pulled out a red construction paper heart. On it Rebecca had drawn a picture of the two of us, hand in hand. "I love you!" she'd printed in big, bold letters.

Rebecca's love notes prompted me to search for some tangible ways of sharing *my* love. I telephoned my foster brother in California to say, "I wish we could be together more often." I made raisin "valentines" on the kids' cereal. (They thought it was silly, but liked it.) I invited an elderly friend who lives alone to be my "mother" for the church Mother-Daughter Banquet.

Are there love notes *you* can share? They'll be appreciated not only on Valentine's Day, but throughout the year. Why, you might even surprise your child (or parent or spouse) with a treasure hunt that ends with a special expression of your love!

—PENNEY SCHWAB

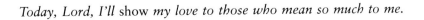

*Today, Lord, I'll show my love to those who mean so much to me.*

*Love. . .is not jealous. . .*
—I Corinthians 13:4 (GNB)

**B**orn in Korea, she was a little, dark-haired baby whose mother could not keep her. But her mother gave her a name that she hoped would be prophetic. She called her newborn daughter *Myung-He,* which means "happiness in the future."

My friend Denise and her husband were lucky enough to adopt Myung-He. Denise wanted to honor her daughter's Korean name, but she also wanted a name that wouldn't set her apart from other American children. Finally, she found an American name that had a similar meaning: Hollie, which means "good luck in the future."

I admire Denise for the love and compassion she showed in choosing that name for her daughter. She was not jealous or threatened by the natural mother's love. Indeed, Denise somehow seemed to multiply it. I believe Hollie one day will understand the love both mothers had in choosing those names.

What a great lesson: welcoming *outside* love for those we love. I will remember Hollie the next time I feel jealous or possessive: when a female coworker shows obvious admiration for my husband, for example; or when my close friend has been graced by yet another friend. Instead of begrudging these feelings of affection, I will try to embrace and honor them, as Denise embraced the love that a young Korean mother had for a daughter whom she gave up to a bright, hopeful future far, far away.

—Terry Helwig

*Lord, help me to understand that a loving heart multiplies instead of divides.*

*Counsel is mine, and sound wisdom: I am understanding; I have strength.*
—PROVERBS 8:14

Sometimes young mothers of twins telephone me just to talk. They've read my book about my own twins and sometimes when I answer the phone the only thing I hear at first is sobbing.

I've learned to just wait. As expected, the words come tumbling out between sobs and a good nose blowing. "It's hard work and no fun. No one ever told me how difficult it is to be the mother of twins."

Then I give my little speech. "It's still hard even though they're sixteen now. But I'll tell you a secret. Motherhood isn't easy, period. Before we bring our babies home, the hospital should print on their bracelets: 'Watch out. It won't be easy. But hang in there. It's worth it.' "

"Thank you, thank you," the mothers invariably say. "I thought I was the only mother who didn't like her children every day."

"Well," I reply, "you're certainly not alone. Now, how about trying to help some other mother? One will surely cross your path. Don't be afraid to tell her that some days you just blow it and that you feel like running away from time to time."

Is there someone you can comfort today with the wisdom you've gained through trials of your own?

—MARION BOND WEST

*Strengthen me, Father, that I might strengthen another.*

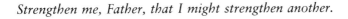

*"Blessed is the man who trusts in the Lord, whose trust is the Lord."*
—JEREMIAH 17:7 (RSV)

When I was a child, spring seemed to take forever in coming. As soon as the April sun began warming the creek, I'd want to go barefoot. Grandma would shake her head "no." Then mild May days would coax blooms from marsh marigolds and trillium. "It's summer!" I'd laugh, tossing my warm sweaters up into the top of the closet. "We ain't had blackberry winter yet," Grandma would say with conviction.

"Blackberry winter"—that's what my grandmother called that final cold snap in May, when blackberries began ripening. And she was always right. Before the month was over, I'd have to retrieve one of those sweaters for a final few days of chilly temperatures.

Now that I'm an adult, I've noticed "blackberry winters" in other areas of my life, too. I save for a vacation, but have to spend the money on a new washer. My "meaningful relationship" with my two teenagers is splintered by occasional spats. I want that recognition for my hard work on the local school board, but am passed over. Sometimes I'm tempted to give up, to surrender to the cynicism that surrounds me. I feel things will never get better.

That's when I think of Grandma, sitting in her rocker, her hands stitching quilting pieces. "It'll never get warm!" I used to whine.

" 'Course it will," she'd laugh. "Blackberry winter is a short season, child. Real short."

And that's the way I try to think of my setbacks, too. Inevitable. Short-lived. As natural as the seasons, the "blackberry seasons" of life.

—MARY LOU CARNEY

*When things don't go the way I want them to, Lord, help me to remember that nothing lasts forever, nothing except Your love and patience.*

*She looketh well to the ways of her household. . . .Her children
arise up, and call her blessed. . .*
—PROVERBS 31:27, 28

Last spring our newspaper printed an unusual photograph of a downtown traffic light. There right inside one of the three cuplike openings was a tiny robin's nest.

This traffic light hung high above one of the busiest intersections in the city. It certainly was not a quiet spot. Horns blared, brakes screeched, and trucks emitted sooty diesel smoke and fumes.

Yet there inside the nest, built right against the bright red light that flashed off and on, day and night, three little fledglings peacefully slept and fed. In the midst of all the noise and clamor, Mother Robin had established a niche of serenity for her family.

My mother did something similar for me. Early in their married life my parents did not have a great deal of security, and there were ups and downs. But had my mother waited for ideal conditions in which to raise a family, I would not be here today. And yet I have carried the fruit of her transforming love and devotion within me all my life. It has sustained me in times of sorrow and blessed me in times of joy. My mother's quiet strength and steadfast faith are a priceless legacy to me.

—ISABEL CHAMP

*Father, I thank You for my mother and for her courage in being mine.*

*If thou canst believe, all things are possible. . .*
—MARK 9:23

As I tucked my seven-year-old daughter in bed, I noticed a sad tilt to her mouth. That afternoon she'd had trouble learning the steps in ballet class and was pulled aside for special help. She was still smarting. "I'm no good, Mama," she said. "I don't think I want to go back."

I patted her hand and opened the book of fairy tales we'd been reading, hoping it would take her mind off the matter.

We read the story of Rapunzel, a beautiful princess who was imprisoned in a tower by a wicked witch. Every day the witch told Rapunzel that she was ugly. Convinced of her ugliness, Rapunzel lost her spirit and gave up hope of leaving the tower. Then one day a prince climbed the tower. Rapunzel saw her image mirrored in his eyes and discovered that she was beautiful. From that moment she was free.

As I closed the book, I thought how easy it was for people to become convinced of their "ugliness," imprisoning themselves in negative thoughts. Maybe they simply needed someone to mirror to them the beauty in their lives.

I looked down at my daughter. "Even the best dancers sometimes take a long time to learn new steps," I said. "You are a beautiful dancer."

"Really?" she asked.

"Really," I said.

Ever so slightly the curve in her mouth lifted. "Maybe I'll go back next week," she said.

—SUE MONK KIDD

*Lord, help me to affirm the gift and possibility I glimpse in the lives around me.*

*What hast thou that thou didst not receive? . . .*
—I CORINTHIANS 4:7

My daughter Karen recently moved back to Kearney, Nebraska, after living away for several years. She lives alone and works full time, so I often invite her to eat lunch with me. Recently, though, she asked me to dinner at her house, and I discovered a surprising thing: I had a rather hard time letting her be the giver! On the way to her house, the thought crossed my mind, "Karen's just making ends meet. I shouldn't eat food that she's bought with her hard-earned money."

Then a memory flashed before my mind. It was my first year of teaching and near the end of the month, so my bank account was running on almost-empty. Mother had come to Kearney to shop, and I'd offered to take her out for lunch, *assuming she'd pick up the tab!* I can still see the blue and white tablecloth under our hands as we both reached for the check. Our eyes met. Mother swallowed hard, smiled and said, "Thank you." I don't think I have ever felt so straight and tall as I did that day as I walked to the cash register and paid the bill. Mother was acknowledging my adulthood! A priceless gift.

When I got to Karen's house, she made me sit down and let her serve me, even though I offered to help. That was hard, but I allowed it because I want her to know how it feels to walk straight and tall.

Do you insist on always being the giver in your relationships? Maybe today you'll have a chance to give the harder gift: letting the other person give to you!

—MARILYN MORGAN HELLEBERG

*Lord, help me to be a gracious receiver.*

*"How forceful are honest words!"*
—JOB 6:25 (RSV)

When my daughter Ann entered her teens, we went through a brief but stormy adjustment period. One morning she came out of her room wearing an odd combination of clothes. "You're not going to school like *that,* are you?" I asked.

She planted her feet. "I was planning on it!" I insisted she change. She resisted. Our voices rose. Before she left we were both practically in tears.

Later when my friend Betty called, I mentioned the episode. "Be honest," she said. "Was it really her choice of clothes that was bothering you?"

*Sure it was,* I thought. But all day the question needled me. Finally I sat in Ann's room and tried to figure it out. As I stared at her closet, I remembered how I used to dress her myself, wrestling her ponytail through turtleneck sweaters. . . I bit my bottom lip, pierced with sadness and longing. That's when my honest moment came. I knew my daughter was just trying to discover her independence. That, after all, was the messy task of adolescence. What was *really* bothering me was that she was growing up.

That evening I revealed my honest moment to Ann. "Be patient with me," I said. "It's hard letting go."

"I know, Mama," she said. "It's hard for me, too. Sometimes I wish I was still small enough for you to dress." Then she wound her arms around me and squeezed tight.

—SUE MONK KIDD

*Dear God, help me to seek honest moments with myself, so I can find them with others.*

*But Jesus said, Suffer little children, and forbid them not,*
*to come unto me: for of such is the kingdom of heaven.*
—MATTHEW 19:14

"Honey, I'm busy now," I told my daughter, and promptly sent her from my kitchen. I had invited guests for dinner that evening and nothing could hinder me like a curious two-year-old.

"Me cook too!" she protested. "Not now," I stated firmly. With a sad look on her face, she toddled off to her daddy in the den.

I worked quickly, tossing the salad and setting the table. I reached into the china cabinet and gently lifted the pink-flowered serving plate. I used the plate only on rare occasions. It was special—given to me by my grandmother.

Standing there holding the plate, I thought back to my childhood and to my grandmother's tiny kitchen. Often, I had stood by her side while she cooked. Every few minutes, she would stop, reach down, and feed me small bites of cabbage and cornbread—my very favorite food! I loved the hours we spent together there, cooking, baking, and best of all, talking. The kitchen had been our "together place," and she had always made me feel welcome.

Then a thought startled me. "Years from now," I asked myself, "what will my daughter remember about me and my kitchen?"

I placed the plate on the table, and headed toward the den to retrieve Alyce. For now I knew that a late dinner would long be forgotten, but a warm "kitchen memory" would last forever.

—DENISE GEORGE

*O Lord, please let me be for my children—and others—the maker*
*of memories warm and plentiful.*

*Truthful lips endure for ever. . .*
—Proverbs 12:19 (RSV)

Brenda is thirteen. "Frienda Brenda," I call her. She's a blond dynamo— full of big plans and ideas, not all of which fly. Take last summer: She figured she'd save half-price on admission to the Alaska State Fair by passing herself off as twelve. Her plan was tempting, I'll admit—our fun money was limited—but the *Wrong Way* warning flashed in my mind and I firmly told her, "No."

A month later, Brenda sat in English class and cheated on a vocabulary test by furtively looking up a definition. All weekend it bothered her. On Monday, she confessed to the teacher. The first I knew of it was the paper she handed me marked with a glaring red F, softened by the instructor's scribbled, "Thanks for being honest."

Honesty costs. . . but it buys a clear conscience. And honesty is hereditary —we parents tend to pass it on to our kids! That *Wrong Way* signal I caught back at the state fair is the same one that kept Brenda truthful—alone and on her own—in the classroom.

Do we want teens who live with integrity? Then you and I must first choose to walk straight ourselves. It's God's High Way and it works. . . honest!

—Carol Knapp

*Father of Truth, thank You for posting those WRONG WAY warnings that keep us moving in the right direction.*

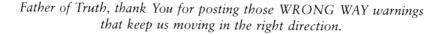

ANTHONY DASILVA

Augustsun shimmered on the stalks of corn, their thick blades rising like endless green walls. My hoe made hollow sounds in the dirt; sweat trickled down my nose. When I reached the end of the row, I went to sit beside Grandma, who was breaking beans in the shade of the snowball bush.

"I'll never get done!" I pouted.

" 'Course you will," she said, her hands methodically snapping bean after bean.

I watched her for a minute and then asked, "Grandma, how many beans have you broken in your life?"

She laughed, piling her apron with yet another batch to break. "Three or four million, I reckon."

"Seems like I have about that many hills of corn to hoe," I grumbled, rubbing the callouses forming on my palms.

Grandma stopped work and laid her hand lightly on my knee. "It's all in how you look at it, child. I never think about the bushels and bushels of beans that need breaking. I just think about the next bean. And then the next. One bean at a time is all I have to break." Her eyes were bright behind her bifocals. "By the yard it's hard; by the inch it's a cinch!"

I remember Grandma's advice—when I have four pies to bake for the church bazaar, when my daughter Amy Jo volunteers me to type her class's literary magazine, when every window in my house needs washing, when I pledge to read the entire Bible in a year, when weeds threaten to repopulate my petunia patch. *By the yard it's hard; by the inch it's a cinch.* Then little by little, one by one, I find I can finish my tasks—just as I did those corn rows so long ago.

—MARY LOU CARNEY

*Sometimes I feel so overwhelmed, Father, by the things I must do.*
*Give me discretion in my commitments. Today, teach me to take small*
*bites of responsibility—to do the inch, and see it's a cinch.*

*"The Lord does not look at the things man looks at. Man looks at the outward appearance, but the Lord looks at the heart."*
—I SAMUEL 16:7 (NIV)

Graduation Day. My youngest daughter Becki is standing in front of the full-length mirror with me behind her. We both stare into it as I adjust her collar, secure her cap, drape the stole around her neck that signifies her high grade point average, attach the gold pin for lifetime membership in the state honor society and hang a bronze medallion around her neck that shows she's graduating cum laude.

Suddenly, the image of my daughter standing proudly in her cap and gown is replaced with the image of a frightened three-year-old in a wheelchair. I see a parade of doctors declaring, "She has cerebral palsy! She'll never walk!" Meanwhile a host of social workers are busily stamping "Unadoptable!" across her files. But God gave us a glimpse of how He saw Becki with her loving demeanor and joyful giggle, and gave us the grace to see past those outward appearances. Becki joined our family.

Looking back, I remember years filled with surgeries, therapy, and lots of hard work and determination from Becki. And now on this day, Becki isn't just graduating. She's *walking* down the aisle to receive her diploma.

Even in the face of what seems to be sorrow and trouble, God blesses us only with good. The secret is in looking with the eyes of the Lord.

—BONNIE WHEELER

*I am thrilled, Lord, by Your handiwork in our lives. Please continue teaching Your powerful lesson on looking past the externals.*

*"Now therefore, our God. . .who keepest covenant and steadfast love. . ."*
—NEHEMIAH 9:32 (RSV)

I admire my seventeen-year-old Tamara. Adventuresome and independent, she creates her own opportunities. And she's loyal . . . to her country, her school, her job, her family. Recently, however, she and I found ourselves in opposing lanes with divided loyalties.

I was away from home when Tam heard a target shooter's gun go off in the woods near our house. Our dog Dandy came yipping through the trees bleeding from a bullet wound. She telephoned the veterinarian, wrapped him in a sheet and very capably made an emergency run to the animal clinic.

The conflict of interest erupted when I arrived on the scene and learned that Dandy's initial medical bill already exceeded two hundred dollars. "We can't afford an injured dog right now!" I wailed.

I considered having him put down. Tam's defiant reaction to this suggestion was a heated, "Do what you want! I don't care! See if I ever try to help a pet again!"

I listened, not to the angry outburst, but to the hurt and betrayal buried beneath. I knew I had to swing a *U-turn* and head in her direction. Why? Because a teenager's trust is not measured in dollars and cents. I would not risk destroying her faith in me by destroying an animal she had tried her best to save. We would do what we could to pull Dandy through.

Loyalty and commitment are powerful travel companions we parents send out with our teens as they journey God's High Way. They hold our kids steady when the going gets slippery. And sometimes, given a chance, the loyalty inside those kids even pulls a faltering parent through.

Dandy, I might add, is fully recovered and continues in his role of loyal family pet.

—CAROL KNAPP

*Faithful Father, Yours is a High Way worth traveling. Keep our eyes steady on Your road signs and our steps securely turned toward You as we walk it with our teens.*

*Thou art . . . an heir of God through Christ.*
—GALATIANS 4:7

After making out my will today, I realized that what I most want to leave my children are things without material value. So here is my *Supplementary Will:*

## ARTICLE I: HOUSE

To each of my children, I hope to leave a home built with the solid bricks of faith in God and self-esteem. May their houses have windows of empathy and doors that open both ways.

## ARTICLE II: VEHICLES

May my children be provided with some means of transportation to take them beyond themselves: an absorbing hobby; a service to others that only they can perform; a talent or favorite recreation that renews their spirit.

## ARTICLE III: PERSONAL ITEMS

I bequeath to each child a jewel box filled with glistening memories: of drinking cocoa by the fire on stormy nights; of *Black Beauty* and *Tom Sawyer* and all the other books that made us laugh and cry together; of the shared miracles of a pumpkin-colored sunset, or tulips sprouting through the snow, or falling stars on a summer night. A bag of tiny diamonds made of little things, such as bedtime kisses, family prayer times and mealtime graces, homemade Valentines, backyard pet shows, penny carnivals and Kool-Aid stands.

## ARTICLE IV: STOCKS AND BONDS

Finally, I would leave my children enough stock in the bonds of love that they will be able to keep investing it in others, becoming "heirs of God through Christ."

## ARTICLE V: TAXES

Before taxes are levied on this estate, please deduct (and forgive) cross words spoken, times of being too busy to listen and missed apologies.

Maybe you'd like to prepare a supplementary will today.

—MARILYN MORGAN HELLEBERG

*Lord, I bequeath these intangibles to those I love:*

_____

_____

_____

*. . . I have learned, in whatsoever state I am, therewith to be content.*
—PHILIPPIANS 4:11

For years grocery shopping was a grueling task. I'd hurry through the store putting anything in sight into my cart. I didn't dare indulge in the luxury of reading labels for fear one of my twin sons would jump out of the cart. My two little daughters would cling to my skirt, making walking cumbersome. One day one of the twins escaped and the manager had to announce over the loudspeaker, "Attention everyone. There is a two-year-old boy with red hair probably hiding in a cardboard box somewhere in the store. All shoppers are requested to look for him." That same day the other twin threw a jar of dill pickles out of the cart and broke it.

I never got accustomed to the icy stares of women with one well-behaved child. I hurriedly admired others who shopped without children. They had grocery lists, organized coupons, manicured nails, and carefully applied makeup, and they strolled leisurely through the grocery store smiling at everyone. So unlike me! *That'll be the day,* I would think to myself.

Now—my children all grown—I grocery shop alone. I can take all the time I want and read labels too. Funny thing. I find myself watching women struggle through the store with whining, rambunctious children and I envy them. I do! I want to go back to the way it used to be. I told my daughter Julie and she happily loaned me her two little ones to take grocery shopping, but she gave me a bit of advice too:

"Mother, you have to be content with who you are in life. Don't look back and yearn for the past," she wisely said. "I love and admire you just the way you are *now!*"

—MARION BOND WEST

*For the changes, adjustments, and wisdom that the years bring, Lord, make me truly thankful for who I am now.*

*The Almighty. . . shall bless thee with blessings of heaven above, blessings of
the deep that lieth under, blessings of the breasts, and of the womb.*
—Genesis 49:25

As a child growing up in the fifties, I was a precocious worry wart. My
mother, seeing my light on late at night, would come into my room
sleepy-eyed, her hair set in bobby pins. "Worrying again?"

"Uh huh," I would nod.

"What about?"

"Well, I didn't do so well on the math test today," I would mumble. It
wasn't true. But I didn't want to tell her the real reason. I had just changed from
a public to a private school. Oh, how I longed to wear cashmere sweaters, just
like the other girls! How I worried that they would laugh at my unstylish
clothes!

My mother would perch on the edge of my bed, cuddling close. "What's
number one on the *Hit Parade?*" she would ask and start singing the latest hit
song without waiting for me to reply. " 'When you're tired and you can't
sleep,' " she crooned softly, just like the record, " 'count your blessings instead of
sheep. . .' "

Then she would say brightly, "Since you're up, you can do what the song
says. Make a Bedtime Blessing List. Writing down all the good things God has
given you will put your mind at ease."

It worked. I hadn't realized that my blessings far outnumbered all the
material things I felt I lacked. My blessings snaked down one page and across
another, and before long my hand was tired, my eyes heavy, and it was all I
could do to ask mother to turn out the light.

—Linda Ching Sledge

*How do You bless me, Lord? Let me count the ways, lest I forget:*

_____

_____

_____

*. . . Forsake not the law of thy mother.*
—PROVERBS 1:8

Fifteen women in sweatsuits jogged up and down the recreation hall to the music of Huey Lewis and the News.

"Your what?" whispered my aerobics teacher as she twirled past.

"My mother," I repeated. "She's visiting this week."

And there she was—67 years old, 122 pounds, scarcely a trace of gray in her thick hair—kicking higher than anyone in the second row.

Mary, the mother of Jesus, often pondered the great mystery of the Child. I have often pondered the great mystery of mothers. My mother is full of surprises—taking up calisthenics after she retired from teaching is the least of these. Every time I think I know her, she'll do or say something that shakes me down to my socks.

The first and only time I didn't make the honor roll, she looked at my sad face and said, "If you think I love you only because you make good grades, you're wrong."

When I brought home a boy who ought to have been every mother's dream—good-looking, rich, well-mannered—she smiled coolly and whispered, "Uh-uh. No imagination."

She was the only one in my family who didn't blanch at my studying for a Ph.D. "I always said you could do better than I," she commented.

It's because of her that I'm taking this aerobics class twice a week. Not that she told me to. But if she can dance, so can (pant, pant) I.

—LINDA CHING SLEDGE

*We thank You, God, for mothers everywhere who push, prod, and prepare us to jump higher than our head, reach farther than our grasp, love wider than our years.*

*Lift up your eyes . . .*
—Isaiah 40:26

"Want to take an after-dinner walk?" my husband David asks.

In my best martyred-fishwife voice I answer, "With half the house left to clean?" To further make my point, I yell down the hall. "Brock! Keri! Don't even think of going to bed until your rooms are cleaned!"

"Oh, Mama," Keri, then six, replies, "we were going to catch lightning bugs."

An hour later, I scan my "things-to-do" list, and see that like last week and the week before, the house is reasonably clean. *Oops, the porch.* Broom in hand, I open the door. The whirr of the vacuum and flying dust have dulled my senses. But one whiff of summer and I'm in another time zone. I think of Keri's lightning bugs, and I recall childhood's cool grass under bare feet and the fresh watermelon smell that hung in the air as I ran through the night reaching for stars. Later, the backyard glider would float like a boat adrift on a secret sea, as I watched luminous lights blinking, blinking, inside a jelly jar.

I walk across the porch, sit on the top step. In the simple dark I take stock. *Do I really want my children to know me as a grouchy mom with a very clean house?*

Summer was offering an alternative. I hurry inside, take four empty jars from under the sink and call my glum family of house-cleaners together. "I have a problem with lightning bugs," I say. "I need to see if it's still fun to catch them on a summer night." And then because confession brightens the soul, I add, "I think it might be more important than a clean house."

It was. It still is.

—Pam Kidd

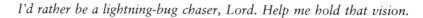

*I'd rather be a lightning-bug chaser, Lord. Help me hold that vision.*

*We love the children of God, when we love God, and keep his commandments.*
—I JOHN 5:2

Once, when I was a very young mother, I took a long train trip with our vivacious four-year-old Mickie. She had napped, but I was very tired. I scolded and fretted as she bounced on the seat, giggled and escaped down the aisle. Catching her, I gave her a spank and told her to sit still and not embarrass me; she was a naughty girl.

I was conscious of a gracious-looking older woman seated across from us, pretending not to notice. But as my little girl cried, she put down her paper and came to us. "May I hold her?" she said gently.

I didn't know whether to be resentful or relieved as I handed my daughter over. At least I could get a little rest. I dozed, and when I woke the train had stopped. The woman was standing beside me, cuddling my child another minute before giving her back. "Raise her with love," she urged kindly. "Never tell her she's bad, praise her. *Raise her with love,*" she repeated.

Picking up her suitcase, the dear lady departed. I never saw her again, but she had left me a priceless gift. Her words became my credo as I raised four children . . . often stilling my voice when I was about to yell, tempering it when I had to scold, saying a prayer when I might explode. I wasn't perfect, far from it, but I learned that children live up to your expectations.

Besides passing those words on to other young mothers over the years, there was one case where I actually interfered. A little boy was being beaten in a department store. "Don't!" I pleaded with his mother. *"Raise him with love."*

To my surprise, she began to cry. She was just a girl herself. "I'm so *tired!*" she wailed.

"I know," I told her, and put my arms around her. I cuddled her child as we talked, giving the same kind advice I once received: Love your children, praise them, and they will make you proud.

Years later, she found me through an article I'd written, and sent me a letter. She was now happily married, with four children. "Just like you!" she wrote. "And I've become a Christian—I'm raising them with love."

—Marjorie Holmes

*Dear Lord, how grateful I am for that angel on the train who set this chain of love in motion. Bless and help all tired, bewildered mothers.*

*"I am the bright Morning Star."*
—REVELATION 22:16 (TLB)

She was a small girl, eight years old, standing lonely on the sidelines. As the other children took turns, blindfolded, to try whacking down the piñata and the onlookers clapped in tune to the "Mexican Hat Dance," her fingers nervously twisted a corner of her dress. It was the PTA's annual school Christmas party.

This year I was responsible for filling the piñata. I had chosen a large pastel star and stuffed it with candies, whistles, snappers and small plastic trinkets. It hung from a rope tossed over a sturdy limb of the elm tree on the playground.

"Don't you want a turn?" I asked the small girl, gingerly urging her forward. "I'll go with you." But she only stood there. *Oh, well,* I thought, *I'll scoop up some candies for her when the piñata gets knocked down.*

After a series of hefty whacks, the star crashed down and split open. Candies and trinkets gushed out to squeals of delight as the children scampered across the playground. Suddenly, without warning, the little girl darted across the grass. From a far corner where it had been carelessly kicked, she picked up the broken star. Clutching it to her heart, she rushed back to me. "Look," she said, "I got the *star!*" She had left the trinkets and treats for the others.

That star endured, perched on one of her bedposts, for several years. I know. You see, she was my little girl.

Let us make the star a celebration of joy each day. When we awaken, let us put our trust in Jesus, *the Morning Star,* our guiding Light. At night, let us call on Christ, our *Evening Star,* Whose presence will light the darkest darkness!

—FAY ANGUS

*Lord, as we reach for the treats, the treasures, the trinkets of life, help us to
remember to reach beyond them for Your star!*

*Save me, O God . . . the floods engulf me . . . You know my folly,*
*O God . . .*
—PSALM 69:1, 2, 5 (NIV)

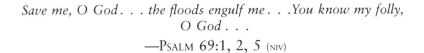

"Hi, Mom, bad news."

Oh, how I hated phone calls from my college student children that started that way! "What is it, Julie?"

"The check I wrote for my tuition bounced!"

The rest of the conversation was one-sided, with me telling her in rather gruff tones that she simply had to start balancing her checkbook every month! She ended up in tears.

The next day I fussed and fumed. *Do I bail her out or let her learn from her mistake?* I was so tormented that finally I decided to make the two-mile drive to Lake Michigan and try to think it out in the solitude I knew I would find there.

Two- to three-foot waves crashed loudly against the sand under immense white clouds. I walked close to the water, skittering back each time a wave rolled up close to my sneakers. Suddenly, one caught me off guard and soaked my shoe, sock and pant leg, making me quite uncomfortable in the fifty-degree weather. From then on I walked farther away from the shoreline—I'd learned my lesson!

And, also, I had found my answer. Julie, too, had been caught "off guard." Perhaps if she had to "walk with wet feet" for a month at college, by living without spending money, she'd learn a lot more about financial responsibility. She could use the money from her part-time job to make good on her tuition check. It would be uncomfortable—but sometimes that's the only way we'll learn.

*Dear Julie,* I thought as I made my way back to my car. *I love you. Try to understand.*

—PATRICIA LORENZ

*Thanks, Lord, that though we sometimes make foolish mistakes, we can always come to You for help. Thank You, too, for calming places of majesty that help put the smaller problems of life back into perspective.*

*And thou shalt be secure . . .*
—JOB 11:18

My daughter Mandy's glassy eyes and red nose affirmed she wasn't feeling well. "I hurt all over," she sighed. I fluffed her pillow, gave her some medicine and tucked the comforter beneath her chin.

"How about some chicken noodle soup?" I asked. She smiled and nodded her approval. Chicken noodle soup was her favorite.

A few minutes later, sitting up in bed, she was slurping away. In between one spoonful, she paused, looked my way and said enthusiastically, "You're the best mom in the whole universe."

I squeezed her hand, thankful she felt secure and loved. I remembered that feeling from when I was a little girl and my mom used to bring me hot tea and toast (my favorite).

As an adult, I often forget that part of me still yearns to be nurtured every now and then. But thanks to a friend's suggestion, I am now doing special little things for myself that evoke warm, secure feelings. Sometimes I light a candle while I write letters. Sometimes I make my favorite cup of tea and snuggle into our wingback chair with an Afghan. Other times I play my favorite tape, buy myself a rose or give myself permission to take a walk in the woods or read—even if all my work *isn't* done.

I'm discovering, like my daughter, that nurturing feels very good. And more likely than not, after I've done something nice for myself, I feel like hugging God and saying with childish enthusiasm, "You're the best God in the whole universe!"

—TERRY HELWIG

*Heavenly Parent, help me nurture that part of me that longs to feel secure and deeply loved by You.*

*Honor thy father and thy mother. . .*
—Exodus 20:12

Last week I took my eighty-one-year-old mother to the Kentucky State Fair. We watched a lamb being groomed for judging, looked at the exhibits and saw border collies display their herding skills. We walked along the midway and enjoyed seeing the children on the merry-go-round. We ate lunch and watched a juggler and a puppet show. It was a good day.

But yesterday she was in what I call one of her "black" moods. She was angry and frantically paced back and forth in her room. She wanted me to take her to see her mother (who died in 1960). She didn't recognize a photo of my father. She accused me of things I had not done.

She has Alzheimer's disease, and both days are characteristic of her behavior nowadays. Sometimes it's as if I'm dealing with an unreasonable child in an adult body.

When the difficult days come, I try to remind myself that this is the same person who so lovingly cared for me when I was a child and was sick or stamped my foot and said, "No." Recalling our past close relationship and the pleasant times we sometimes still have helps me to regain my perspective on the hard days. Even when she's very difficult, it doesn't change the fact that she's my mother and I am committed to being there for her.

—Barbara Chafin

*Lord, help me truly to honor my mother. Grant me love and wisdom and patience on the difficult days.*

*Then they [older women] can train the younger women to love their husbands*
*and children, to be self-controlled and pure. . .*
—TITUS 2:4, 5 (NIV)

"Lord, forgive me. I was a terrible mother today. . ." I started crying before I could pray any further. I had begun the summer with all the enthusiastic plans an energetic young mother could dream up: We had been to the park, the zoo, swim lessons, summer camp and the beach. But by the end of August all that was left were three bored, squabbling kids and their frazzled mother. And now here I was embarrassing myself by breaking down at my women's prayer meeting.

Another young mother followed, "Oh, Lord, I also was so short-tempered with my little Jeannie tonight . . ." Karen started weeping along with me.

Then Betty, a woman in her late forties, started praying for us both. Her children were grown, but she well-remembered those long end-of-summer days with small kids. "Lord, help Bonnie and Karen," Betty began. "Help them to be the godly mothers You want them to be. Comfort them in their need. And, Lord, help them to forgive themselves."

Buoyed by the prayers, understanding and offers of help from the others present, I began to cope much better. Before summer completely ended, the kids and I returned to the park, the zoo and the beach, and my husband and I found time together apart from them, too. I discovered I had a whole lot of love and energy within me, but most of all I learned I didn't have to do it alone.

Are you shouldering a burden or responsibility that is crushing you? Listen to one who foolishly tried to do it alone. Turn to others—a spouse, a friend, a small support group—and share your concern. Let their understanding heal you, let their prayers guide you, and by all means say, "Yes!" to their offers of help.

—BONNIE WHEELER

*Lord, as I grow older and the cycles of my life change, help me to reach out to*
*others with love, understanding and remembrance.*

*Thou shalt forget thy misery . . .*
—JOB 11:16

A lthough my Grandma Rae was housebound because of severe arthritis, she never let it get her down. She was well-read, informed on news events and through TV was up on all the latest trends. Visitors dropped by daily, myself included. One time a friend came to spend an hour cheering up Grandma. But it seemed that all she wanted to do was complain—about the weather, about a lazy husband, about a son who didn't visit often, about. . .

Grandma listened patiently, but when the woman began listing *Grandma's* troubles ("Oh, you poor dear, you can't walk"), Grandma put a stop to that right away. "I make it a point," she said firmly, "to forget my troubles as easily as most folks forget their blessings."

I remember being shocked at Grandma's blunt words and wondering how her friend would take them. But after a short pause, the woman laughed and began talking about the pleasure she got from her gardening and other hobbies!

I've always remembered these words. They come to me whenever I'm tempted to let my troubles cloud out a clear and sunny day.

—LINDA NEUKRUG

*Dear God, let me be as quick to forget my troubles as I tend to be at forgetting my blessings. And help me to remember Your goodness always.*

*Draw near to God and he will draw near to you. . .*
—JAMES 4:8 (RSV)

"Mom, please don't go." Twelve-year-old Kendall gripped my arm as we stood by the car in the camp parking lot that summer Sunday afternoon. Her voice quivered and her eyes filled with tears. "I'm *scared.*"

Any mother who's heard those words from her child knows the instinctive response. I wanted to wrap my arms around her, to comfort and protect her from her fears. But almost as instinctively, I knew I should not.

Kendall has always been our homebody, even reluctant to spend the night with friends because she gets homesick. Yet she bravely decided to try this week-long church camp experience in the mountains. "I *know* you'll be okay," I said, kissing the top of her head and trying to sound confident in spite of my own shaky emotions.

"How do you *know?*" she begged, hoping for some assurance that would help her right now.

"I just do," I replied. "Jesus will be with you."

At that moment, a counselor and some kids walked by. "C'mon, Kendall!" they called. She seemed immobile, torn between wanting to go and wanting to stay. So I made the first move. "Good-bye, sweetie," I said, hugging her and then quickly getting into the car and driving away without looking back. All the way down the mountain, I ached for Kendall, but I kept remembering the words of a wise friend: "Sometimes our children learn to depend upon the Lord only when we get out of the way."

Throughout the long week, I didn't know who was suffering most, but when I picked up Kendall on Saturday, she came running to the car and I got my answer. "Mom, this was the *best* week of my life!"

—CAROL KUYKENDALL

*Lord, may I learn to get out of the way when You want to teach my children to depend upon You.*

*For none of us liveth to himself. . .*
—ROMANS 14:7

One day I was walking along the street with a friend and as we approached a florist shop, he said, "Let's go in here for a moment. I want to send my mother some flowers."

"Oh," I said, "is it her birthday?"

"No," he replied, "it's mine."

"And you're sending your mother flowers?"

"Yes," he nodded. "It's a way to thank her for giving me life and for taking care of me all those years until I could take care of myself."

I thought that was a very touching gesture, and it made good sense to me. Living far from my own family, I had always sent my mother a gift on her birthday, on Mother's Day, her wedding anniversary, and at Christmas, but it had never occurred to me to send her anything on *my* birthday, and for such good reasons. So the next time my birthday came around, I sent my mother some flowers.

That evening she telephoned. "What's all this about?" she asked.

"It's my birthday," I said.

"I know that. Did you get my card?"

"Yes," I said. "Thanks. And the flowers are just to thank you for giving me life and taking care of me all those years until I could take care of myself."

Silence. I could almost see her fighting back the tears. Then in that way she has always had of brushing aside gratitude and praise, she said, "Well, I'm glad you finally noticed."

—GLENN KITTLER

*Father, the Source of all life, teach us to be mindful of those who love us and through whom Your gifts of life and blessings flow.*

*"But seek the welfare of the city where I have sent you . . . for in its welfare you will find your welfare."*
—JEREMIAH 29:7 (RSV)

"Kendall, I will *never ever* do this again," I vowed through clenched teeth to my thirteen-year-old daughter as we scraped paper off the walls of her bedroom. Pulling this little-girl paper off and putting up something more appropriate for a teenager represented a rite of passage for Kendall and she was clearly excited. But I detested the tedious task and had been complaining for two solid days as we worked away.

"But, Mom," Kendall offered, "it's going to look so good!"

"I hope so," I muttered, spraying more water on a new section, "because it's going to stay on these walls *forever.*"

The next day, I ran into the mother of one of Kendall's friends who asked what we'd been up to lately. Immediately, I launched into an exaggerated description of the pains of peeling wallpaper.

"Oh, Mandy and I did that a few weeks ago," she answered. "We laughed and talked about growing up. . . stuff we never sit down and discuss. I was glad for the opportunity."

We parted laughing, but as I turned to walk away, I was almost in tears. Same job. Different attitude. And certainly, a different result: She seized upon an *opportunity* I totally missed because of my whining and complaining.

I wonder if Martha felt the same regret when she realized she missed the *opportunity* of sitting at the feet of Jesus in her own living room because of her fussing and complaining. I also wonder if Kendall might like to re-wallpaper her room again in a couple of years.

Then again, maybe we'll find other *opportunities . . .*

—CAROL KUYKENDALL

*Lord, I want to learn from my mistakes. May I turn regret over missed opportunities into lessons for next time.*

THE AFRICA

*For we know not what we should pray for as we ought: but the Spirit itself maketh intercession for us with groanings which cannot be uttered.*
—ROMANS 8:26

I was a young teen then thoroughly uninterested in house chores. The ironing board wobbled and groaned as I drove the iron into the shirt collar one more time. It crinkled even more.

"Your trouble is that you're working too hard," Grandma said, taking the iron. "You let the heat do the work, not all that pushing and pressing." Almost effortlessly, she ironed the collar smooth.

That happened a long time ago, but I thought of it again on a recent hectic day. I had run to the window for the hundredth time to check my toddler, then back to folding laundry. Could I get Breton to piano lessons and back in time to baby-sit? And what about the PTA? By afternoon, stress weighed heavily on me like an overloaded backpack.

Suddenly I could see Grandma taking the iron: "All that pushing and pressing!" I should be letting the Holy Spirit do the work! Wasn't that what "casting all your care upon Him" (I Peter 5:7) was about?

Sure enough, as I made time to pray for help, I found that the still small Voice was present: "Your husband would be willing to help with the driving. Don't be so worried about telling the PTA 'No' this time." Before I knew it, my day's work was done, and I even had time to relax that evening with my family.

Are you working too hard today? Remember Grandma's words: "Let the heat do the work."

—KATHIE KANIA

*Lord, help me remember that Your burden is light when carried in the Spirit.*

*. . .This is my beloved Son: hear him.*
—Mark 9:7

One day while shopping in a department store, my small daughter began one of those long, wandering stories children sometimes tell. Her words buzzed around my ears like a worrisome fly, something about her friend's hamster. "Uh huh," I muttered absently, my mind on my shopping list. I didn't even pause as I made my way down the aisle. Finally she grew quiet.

On the way home, we stopped at an ice-cream shop. At the next table sat a mother and a little boy, each holding a cone. He was recounting a lengthy school tale to her, and there were big, familiar-sounding gaps where nothing came out except "and . . . and . . . and . . ." But what absolutely amazed me was that his strawberry ice cream dropped steadily from the cone onto his hand and spread to the cuff of his shirt as he talked—yet his mother never interrupted to wipe it off. She simply looked into his face and listened to his words as though each one was the most important word in the world.

I had a strange feeling that God was purposely reminding me of something I desperately needed to hear. When I am too busy to pause and pay attention to what someone is saying to me, no matter how trivial it may seem, I am sending a message of how unimportant I think that someone is. With a start I realized that listening—*really* listening with focused ears and open heart—is a way of loving.

I turned to Ann. "What was that about the hamster, honey?"

—Sue Monk Kidd

*When someone speaks to me today, Lord, help me to stop,*
*look, listen—and love.*

*And thine ears shall hear a word . . . saying, This is the way,*
*walk ye in it . . .*
—Isaiah 30:21

The wait in the maternity section of the hospital approached nine-and-a-half hours. My daughter Julie, along with her husband Rick, were behind the swinging doors that read "Labor and Delivery." Our families waited. Perhaps they, like I, tried not to remember two years ago when we'd been in this same situation. Julie had given birth to a son who had not cried at birth. Robbie lived only twenty-five minutes. No one, except God, knew of my desperate need to hear this grandchild's first cry.

I was nearly asleep in one of the waiting room chairs at twelve-thirty in the morning, when I thought God gave me some unusual instructions. *Go and get yourself a cup of coffee.*

*I don't drink coffee,* I thought. The message came again, urging me softly, gently. Not understanding at all, I went through the swinging doors into the labor and delivery area where the coffeepot was located. Family members had been invited to help themselves to coffee throughout the wait. As I poured a cup, I noticed on the giant blackboard that Julie was the only patient who hadn't delivered. I stirred cream and sugar into my coffee, feeling quite foolish. Then, the unmistakable, sudden, beautiful wail of a newborn pierced the silent night. *That's my grandchild!* Now I understood why I had this nudge to come to the coffee room.

Grateful, rejoicing, amazed, nearly dancing down the empty hall, I hurried back to the waiting room. The house phone was ringing and I answered it. "Mama! Mama!" the familiar voice laughed and cried uncontrollably. "We have a son! A little boy! Perfect! Thomas is here!" *I know,* I thought, silently rejoicing with her. I brought the coffee cup to my lips. I drank the best cup of coffee I've ever had, as I thanked my Father for my new grandson and for His remarkable instructions.

—Marion Bond West

*Father, help me forget all reason and logic when You tell me to do something,*
*and simply obey You.*

*And let the peace of God rule in your hearts. . . .and be ye thankful.*
—COLOSSIANS 3:15

It's Saturday morning. I am in my kitchen listening to the coffeemaker bubble and hiss, and the refrigerator whine. In a few minutes, three alarm clocks will buzz and my menfolk will tumble out of bed clamoring for breakfast. Another busy day will begin.

Every day is busy for a working mother. Sometimes I feel like a computer on overload, crammed full of the data of four lives: nursery school projects; homework schedules; which child needs new clothes and which can go awhile without his seams bursting; the telephone numbers of three good friends willing to watch sick kids at a moment's notice.

I am so used to moving at top speed that it is hard to wind down and rest. Sometimes I resent the demands and the overload. Sometimes I'm angry. Sometimes sad, because I don't feel appreciated.

Yet I know that, alone and idle, I am empty.

The coffeemaker gives one last groan. The thick brown drops fall slower and slower. The refrigerator clanks into silence. I can almost hear the mist caught in the branches of the silver beech tree losing itself in the morning air. Suddenly, You are with me, nearer than my breathing, closer than my beating heart.

Three pairs of feet come clomping downstairs. Three voices sing out to me. I get the skillet and pour myself some coffee. It feels like a French toast morning.

—LINDA CHING SLEDGE

*Dear Lord, I need these quiet moments with You to remember
how my cup runneth over.*

*He heals the brokenhearted . . .*
—PSALM 147:3 (RSV)

An amazing discovery for me recently has been that in all adults there is still the child whose spirit was wounded somehow when quite small. For my oldest child Julie, a wound recently surfaced. When she was in second grade, I didn't prepare her attractive school lunches or even buy her a lunch box. I'd just had twin sons and mornings were hectic. Just recently she confessed that she often ate alone because she was embarrassed by her lunches. Thirty-year-old Julie already had children of her own when I found out about her childhood hurt. I stood in stores looking fondly at lunch boxes, wishing, longing for another chance.

Then, one day, I happened to find an old lunch box from the sixties, the time when Julie was in school. I admired it so much that the owner gave it to me. I packed goodies for Julie, some candy and gum and her favorite cosmetics, but mainly little treasures—an antique pin, an old lace handkerchief, very old paper dolls, a small book published in the 1800s. Of course, the long overdue note that she had so wanted to find in her lunch back in 1968 went in. "Julie Babe, have a good day. I love you. Mama." I mailed the carefully wrapped lunch box for its thousand-mile trip. *Could a lunch box more than twenty years late possibly ease the silent pain she endured?*

Her letter came immediately. "Mother, I never realized I'm still seven years old. It was so emotionally heavy I could barely breathe. It was just like I was sitting at the long lunch table and could even smell school when I opened the lunch box. All my friends were there and watched me. As I walked back through my second-grade lunch experience, I thought, *Mama does care. I am important.*"
—MARION BOND WEST

*Keep reminding me, Father, that often healing a long-ago hurt can be quite simple. Amen.*

*Know how to give good gifts. . . .*
—MATTHEW 7:11

This past year, when scattered children and grandchildren came home, my oldest son produced a special treat: our old movies of Christmases past, all of which he'd transferred to videotape.

Mark turned on the set, and laughing and pointing, we sat reliving the merry commotion: hanging up stockings; trimming the tree; rescuing the cat from its tangle of tinsel; church pageants and plays; little angels singing; bathrobed shepherds waving as they marched onstage; Mickie dancing in *The Nutcracker Suite*.

Then, when the show was over, they all began to discuss other Christmases. "Remember the years we adopted some poor family? How everybody got busy making or buying presents. You and Daddy let us pick out the turkey, and we were so proud, but one time Mallory dropped it in the mud. Sure wish we had a shot of that!"

"Me, too," his sister spoke up. "But what I remember most are those Raggedy Anns and Andys we made. I helped Mother sew them, you younger kids did the stuffing and she took you along to deliver them. Boy, were you excited!"

"I was selfish," Melanie confessed. "I wanted to keep my Andy. But I was never so thrilled as when I handed him over!"

On and on they went, recalling things I'd almost forgotten. And listening, I suddenly noticed: Not once did they mention anything they got. Not even a first bicycle or special doll. Instead, to my surprise, the memories they treasured most were the fun they had in giving.

"Oh, Mother," Melanie was laughing, "doing things like that was the best part of Christmas."

"It sure was," the others agreed, expressing only one regret: How nice it would be now to see movies of those times, too.

Then several of them expressed it: Yes, but we didn't need them. We were doing something more important. The pictures were already engraved on our hearts.

—MARJORIE HOLMES

PELLEGRINI

*Dear Lord, we weren't perfect parents. You know how often we failed our children; how miserable we often were, worrying about gifts we couldn't buy them. But now my heart overflows with thanksgiving. To realize we did give them something money couldn't buy or any camera record—the sheer wonder and joy of giving!*

*And when he had sent the multitudes away,*
*he went up into a mountain apart to pray. . .*
—MATTHEW 14:23

It was one of Mother's rules. Every day, when we were little, she made us stay in our rooms, by ourselves, for about twenty minutes. "I needed to get you out of my hair," she later explained. Actually she was following the advice of some long-forgotten child psychologist she had read in a magazine. The point was that children should learn to entertain themselves. They should know the pleasures of being alone.

I can still recall those quiet afternoons when I watched the eucalyptus trees outside my window quaking in the breeze. I can remember seeing the ocean from a rented beach house, sunlight scattered on the sea like glitter spilled from a bottle. I can recall quiet times of creating cartoons out of cracks on my bedroom ceiling and making pictures out of the long shadows cast on my linoleum floor. I learned to enjoy being alone.

I've heard it said that we need to be quiet for God to speak to us—we need to be empty of the projects, schemes, worries and doubts that get in the way of His working through us. When Jesus needed to be closer to God He always sought some time alone.  When I feel far from God, I try to do the same. . . putting into practice a lesson my mother taught long ago.

—RICK HAMLIN

*Lord, give me solitude when I need it*
*so that I may hear Your Word.*

*Her children shall be nursed at her breasts, carried on her hips and dandled on her knees. I will comfort you there as a little one is comforted by its mother.*
—ISAIAH 66:12–13 (TLB)

The most wonderful card I ever received was the handmade, beautifully painted Father's Day card my daughter Jeanne sent me for Father's Day a few years after I became a single parent. I'd been both mother and father to her, she wrote, and she just wanted me to know how much she appreciated it.

Mother's Day is generally an event orchestrated by fathers. They take the kids shopping and help them buy gifts and flowers for Mom. Some husbands take their wives out for brunch to celebrate her special day. But when there's no dad around, a single mom is lucky if a thoughtful teacher has organized the making of a Mother's Day card during art class. Often there's nothing special about that day for her. I once spent the whole day alone.

Think about all the single-parent moms you know. Think about how Mother's Day is in some way the most important day of the year for them, because they aren't wives anymore—only mothers. And they usually do it while holding down full-time jobs and trying to make ends meet.

Ask if you can "borrow" the children of a single-parent mom for a few hours. Take them shopping for gifts for their mother—not expensive ones, but something she can unwrap excitedly. Help the children wrap the gifts, if necessary. The children will be excited about the whole idea. But that mother—she'll appreciate it more than you can imagine.

—PATRICIA LORENZ

*Jesus, You loved and honored Your mother. Please help me not only to honor my own mother, but to make life a little special for a mother who is raising her children alone.*

*"Let not thy left hand know what thy right hand doeth."*
—MATTHEW 6:3

A friend whose mother lived with her during the last years of her life wrote in her Christmas letter, "I haven't sent out Christmas cards since 1987, when Mom was still with me. She always wanted to help make my life easier, so I set her to work putting stamps and return address stickers on the envelopes. It really saved me a *lot* of time. She fixed many more envelopes than I needed, and this year when I got out my Christmas things, there they were! So I'm using them (twenty-two-cent stamps and all!) and am *again* being saved a lot of time. I feel Mom's presence as I write cards and am warmed by the knowledge that, nearly two years after her death, she is still smoothing the way and making life easier for me. (She would be *so* pleased at that!)"

What a lovely surprise for my friend! It made me wonder what seeds I might plant to be discovered later (after I'm gone, or next week, tomorrow or a month from now) by those I love. For example, my daughter has a friend who secretly plants bulbs (tulip, iris, gladiolus) in the yards of her friends. Then, early in the spring, beautiful flowers appear in their yards, bringing them great delight and a feeling of being loved.

What could you and I do today to surprise those we love tomorrow? Send someone a magazine subscription without a notification card? Hide love notes in sock drawers, or car glove compartments, or in the family Bible? Consider it a special secret between God and you. It will make you feel closer to Him as well as to those you want to surprise!

—MARILYN MORGAN HELLEBERG

*Friend Jesus, please join me in planning—and planting—some secret surprises for my dear ones.*

Copyright © 1994 by Guideposts Associates, Inc., Carmel, NY 10512.

This 1994 edition published by Crescent Books, distributed by Outlet Book Company, Inc., A Random House Company, 40 Engelhard Avenue, Avenel, New Jersey, 07001.

Random House
New York • Toronto • London • Sydney • Auckland

*Book design by Kathryn W. Plosica*

All Scripture quotations, unless otherwise noted, are from the King James or Authorized Version of the Bible.

Quotations marked RSV are from the *Revised Standard Version of the Bible,* copyright © 1946, 1952, 1971 by the Division of Christian Education of the National Council of the Churches of Christ in the United States of America and are used by permission.

Quotations marked NIV are from the *New International Version of the Bible,* copyright © 1978 by New York International Bible Society, and are used by permission.

Quotations marked TLB are from *The Living Bible,* copyright © 1971 owned by transfer to Illinois Marine Bank N.A. (as trustee). Used by permission of Tyndale House Publisher, Wheaton, IL 60188.

Quotations marked NASB are from *The New American Standard Version of the Bible,* copyright © The Lockman Foundation 1960, 1962, 1963, 1968, 1971, 1972, 1973, 1975, and are used by permission.

Quotations marked GNB are from *The Good News Bible: The Bible in Today's English Version.* Copyright © American Bible Society, 1966, 1971, 1976.

Quotations marked JB are from the *Jerusalem Bible.* Copyright © 1966 by Darton, Longman & Todd, Ltd., and Doubleday, a division of Bantam Doubleday Dell Publishing Group, Inc.

All material appeared originally in *Daily Guideposts.* Copyright © 1983, 1984, 1986, 1987, 1988, 1989, 1990, 1991, 1992 by Guideposts Associates, Inc., Carmel, New York 10512.

*Special thanks* to the following people who generously volunteered photos for this book: Tracy Allocco, Debra Borg, Harold Clarke, Joyce DaSilva, Edward Davis, Andrea Ward-Guidry, Lillian Guzzo, Mary Helen Joscelyne-Fink, Carolyn Markowitz, Sue Malone-Barber, Gene Miller, Jeanne Mosure, Shelley Ortner, Ron Palmer, Rebecca Pasko, Bruno and Nina Pellegrini, Ellen Reed, Melissa Ring, Yvette Romero, Paul Small, Jane Susswein and Caroline Wolgast.

**Library of Congress Cataloging-in-Publication Data**

Celebrations of a Mother's Love : real stories from Guideposts about mothers and their children.
    p.  cm.
   ISBN 0-517-10104-1 : $9.99
   1. Motherhood—Religious aspects—Christianity—Meditations. 2. Mothers—Prayer-books and devotions—English. I. Guideposts (Pawling, N.Y.)
BV4529.M68     1994
242'.6431—dc20
                                     93-39468
                                        CIP